Unlocking the Secrets of Science

Profiling 20th Century Achievers in Science, Medicine, and Technology

Albert Einstein and the Theory of Relativity

John Bankston

PO Box 619 • Bear, Delaware 19701
www.mitchelllane.com

Unlocking the Secrets of Science

Profiling 20th Century Achievers in Science, Medicine, and Technology

Albert Einstein and the Theory of Relativity

Printing   1   2   3   4   5   6   7   8   9   10

Library of Congress Cataloging-in-Publication Data
Bankston, John, 1974-
    Albert Einstein and the theory of relativity/John Bankston.
      p. cm. — (Unlocking the secrets of science)
    Summary: A biography of the physicist whose theories of relativity revolutionized the way we look at space and time.
    Includes bibliographical references and index.
    ISBN 1-58415-137-4 (lib. bdg.)
    1. Einstein, Albert, 1879-1955—Juvenile literature. 2. Relativity (Physics)—Juvenile literature. 3. Physicists—Biography—Juvenile literature. [1. Einstein, Albert, 1879-1955. 2. Physicists. 3. Relativity (Physics)] I. Title. II. Series.
QC16.E5 B34 2002
530'.092—dc21
[B]   2002066068

ABOUT THE AUTHOR: Born in Boston, Massachusetts, John Bankston began publishing articles in newspapers and magazines while still a teenager. Since then, he has written over two hundred articles, and contributed chapters to books such as *Crimes of Passion* and *Death Row 2000*, which have been sold in bookstores around the world. He has recently written a number of biographies for Mitchell Lane including books on Mandy Moore, Jessica Simpson, Jonas Salk, and Alexander Fleming. He currently lives in Portland, Oregon.

CHILDREN'S SCIENCE REVIEW EDITOR: Stephanie Kondrchek, B.S. Microbiology, University of Maryland

PUBLISHER'S NOTE: In selecting those persons to be profiled in this series, we first attempted to identify the most notable accomplishments of the 20th century in science, medicine, and technology. When we were done, we noted a serious deficiency in the inclusion of women. For the greater part of the 20th century science, medicine, and technology were male-dominated fields. In many cases, the contributions of women went unrecognized. Women have tried for years to be included in these areas, and in many cases, women worked side by side with men who took credit for their ideas and discoveries. Even as we move forward into the 21st century, we find women still sadly underrepresented. It is not an oversight, therefore, that we profiled mostly male achievers. Information simply does not exist to include a fair selection of women.

Contents

Probably the most famous scientist the world has ever known, Albert Einstein waited years before his theories were accepted—or even understood!

Chapter 1

Scientist Superstar

. . . .

He was famous. When he was alive he was as well known as a movie star, as respected as any star athlete. Strangers approached him on the street seeking autographs, newspaper photographers snapped his picture. He was probably the most famous scientist of the 20th century, perhaps the most famous scientist who ever lived. Once on a bet two British scientists mailed a postcard with just his name and *United States* for an address. The postcard reached him without delay. In later life, despite a lifetime of avoiding politics, he was offered the presidency of the newly formed country of Israel.

Today, although he's been dead for about half a century, his picture adorns the rooms of thousands of scientists and nonscientists alike. His image has been tacked up in as many dormitories and bedrooms as that of another icon, James Dean—who also died in 1955. But while Dean was celebrated for his youth and tragic early death, this scientist was revered for his intellect and for changing our view of the universe. James Dean became famous because of his movie *Rebel Without a Cause*. This scientist was also a rebel, but he had a cause.

His theories were constructed when he was in his mid-20s, but few believed them, and even fewer understood them. During a scientific meeting in 1919, J.J. Thomson said of one such theory, "This is the most important result obtained in connection with the theory of gravity since Newton's day. It is one of the highest achievements of human thought."

Astronomy professor Arthur Eddington was an early believer in Einstein's theories.

Afterward astronomy professor Arthur Eddington was stopped by a man who asked him if it was true, if the astronomer was one of only three people in the entire world who understood this famous scientist's theories. When Eddington paused for a moment, the man reportedly said, "Don't be modest, Eddington." "Not at all," the professor replied. "I was wondering who the third might be."

Before the 20th century, the greatest advances in science and medicine came from observation and experimentation. Indeed, Sir Isaac Newton is said to have discovered his famous theory of gravity when an apple fell from a tree and whacked him on the head. By the 18th and 19th centuries, steady improvements in the power of microscopes enabled scientists to examine once invisible microscopic organisms. While these instruments expanded scientists' view of life on Earth, the telescope's increasing power changed their view of the universe around our planet.

As the 19th century faded, scientists gave serious consideration to forces we could not see. Theories developed about light, gravity, and a weightless, invisible substance they called the ether. Light was then viewed as a wave; scientists believed that just as the ocean needed water to carry waves, light needed the ether.

In the early 20th century, one man developed theories that explained many of his contemporaries' questions about the unseen world of gravity and light. His most famous writings demonstrated why light is the "speed limit" for the universe, and what happens when matter is converted into energy. It would take years—even decades—for portions of his theories to be understood. But once they were, they would be used in everything from the development of television to the construction of the atomic bomb.

The famous scientist was Albert Einstein. Even adults with limited scientific backgrounds usually know his name and, even more unusual for a scientist, know what he looked like. He was as famous for his wild gray hair and deep, thoughtful eyes as he was for his simple equation $E = mc^2$. Before his fame he would know poverty, prejudice, and divorce. When he first wrote the theories that changed the way the universe was viewed, he was not a professor at a prestigious university or a respected scientist. He was a lowly patent clerk unable to land a better job. This is his story.

Before he was a respected scientist, Albert was just a quiet, bright boy— and a big brother to Maja, who looked up to him as only a kid sister can.

Chapter 2

Dreams of the Invisible

• •

Hermann Einstein's business was failing. Even in the 1800s, small companies often struggled in competition with larger ones. Hermann's electrical goods business was losing customers to major corporations.

Albert Einstein was born in Ulm, Germany, on March 14, 1879. He was barely a year old when his father, Hermann, uprooted the family. Hermann hoped to somehow succeed in a new city. This would be an impossible dream. Broke, he moved his infant son and wife, Pauline, to Munich. There they lived off the charity of his younger brother, Jakob, and the two men opened a small electrochemical business paid for by Pauline's parents.

Hermann, though financially unsuccessful, was a workaholic; Pauline was the parent who spent the most time with Albert. Albert was her first child, but even if he hadn't been, Pauline probably would have realized how unusual her son was. A sweet-faced boy, even as a toddler Albert owned the eyes of someone whose thoughts were often far away. In later life he would claim that as a baby he practiced forming sentences by himself. He wasn't interested in saying anything until he was capable of holding a conversation. Regardless of whether or not this is true, Albert didn't speak until he was three years old.

At first his parents worried; they were convinced their son was "slow." But before he was five, those concerns began to fade. Pauline was an avid pianist. Her son enjoyed watching her play so much that she enrolled him in violin lessons. While both Albert and his younger sister, Maja, learned how to play the instrument at a young age, Albert was a quicker study—before he entered grade school he was already fairly proficient. He was similar to many other budding geniuses who show an aptitude for musical instruments long before their skills in math or science are recognized.

Spending most of his time with his mother and rarely seeing his father was even less unusual one hundred years ago than it is today. Still, Albert craved his father's attention. The few minutes a day he spent with Hermann were precious and recalled years later. In fact, one such time would change Albert's life.

Albert got sick when he was five years old. It wasn't serious, but he couldn't go out to play. He was restless and unhappy. His mood changed when his father came in his room. Hermann brought a compass, probably thinking it would amuse his son to play with it. Albert was fascinated as his father slowly turned the instrument in his hand. No matter what direction the compass was turned to, the needle always pointed north. But why? Albert asked (Albert was always asking why, a habit he never outgrew).

Hermann was able to manage an explanation about magnetism, but when Albert asked how magnetism was able to cross through space, Hermann was stumped. That night, despite his illness, Albert couldn't sleep. He imagined an invisible force that could go through walls. It would be the first of many riddles about the invisible world to grab his attention. Because his father had introduced the problem, it became even more important.

Many math and science prodigies gain early attention for their musical abilities. Albert Einstein was a talented violinist as a child, and he continued to play throughout his life.

Albert loved and admired his father and would later call him "wise," one theory he'd have a hard time proving. Still, for all his flaws, Hermann encouraged Albert's fascination with the mysterious. Albert spent much of his childhood struggling to unravel mysteries like magnetism. Unfortunately the schools he attended discouraged his natural curiosity.

The Einsteins were Jewish at a time in Germany's history when Jewish people were enjoying a taste of freedom. Before the 1870s, German laws dictated everything in Jewish life, from the number of Jewish people who were allowed to marry each year to where they could live. While many people are aware of the tremendous horrors German Jews suffered in the 1930s and '40s, most don't realize how difficult it was being Jewish in Germany only a short time before Albert's birth. The time period in which he grew up was a special one indeed, a brief pause between two different forms of government that sought to reduce or even eradicate the Jewish population.

Hermann wasn't a religious man, but he made sure that Albert received a religious education at home. Still, when Albert turned seven, his father sent him to a Catholic school, believing it offered the best possible education for his son. As the only Jewish child in his class, Albert endured some abuse from his peers, but it was nothing compared to what his teachers dished out.

The school Albert attended, like most German schools then, emphasized discipline and obedience over creative thought. The school was run like a little army, and punishments were often fairly harsh. Albert had a tough time because he hated being told what to do, and he loved to question his teachers.

Today there is a myth about Albert Einstein that he was a mediocre student, but in the beginning this was far from the case. After his first year in school, Albert's mother wrote to his grandmother, "Yesterday Albert received his grades, he was again number one, his report card was brilliant."

In 1889, Albert entered the Luitpold Gymnasium, a school similar to high schools in the United States. A school photograph still exists from Albert's first year at the gymnasium. In it Albert's classmates stand rigid and facing forward, their bodies and expressions suggesting young soldiers in training. Albert looks more relaxed, a mischievous smirk painting his face as if he's getting ready to tell a joke or play a prank—anything except stand in disciplined order waiting for the photographer to do his job.

School was a miserable place for Albert. Home offered a welcome retreat.

Hermann was not the only one to awaken Albert's interest in science and mathematics. Uncle Jakob took the time to introduce him to algebra. Not only did Albert grasp its difficult concepts years before his peers, eventually even his uncle was unable to answer his nephew's questions. At 12, Albert found an even brighter adult to question—medical student Max Talmud, who often joined the Einsteins for a Thursday meal. Talmud began lending young Albert basic science textbooks, but before long the budding scientist had torn through the most advanced texts. Like Uncle Jacob, Max soon found himself unable to answer Albert's questions.

At first, Max tried to solve this by encouraging Albert to study an area where he was more knowledgeable: medicine. Albert wasn't interested. Instead of medicine, Albert took on another discipline—philosophy. It was there, reading borrowed books from Max, that Albert first came across the writings of Immanuel Kant. Kant had constructed an elaborate philosophical system designed to explain how the entire universe functioned. As soon as he read Kant's writings, Albert realized he wanted to use mathematics to accomplish the same thing. As he grew older, he became fascinated by physics—the radical new science that studied matter and energy and the way the two interact.

Just as magnetism fascinated him as a child, by his mid-teens Albert was equally drawn to light. Earlier scientists had described light as a wave, one that traveled on an invisible conductor called ether. Albert began his first thought experiments, imagining what it would be like to ride a beam of light. He pictured looking down upon the earth as he rapidly flew away; he wondered what time would be like and how it would change.

He would go on to write a five-page essay about the ether and send it to his Uncle Caesar. While there was little hint of the later theories Albert would embrace, his uncle was so impressed, he told Pauline that Albert could look forward to an amazing future.

Unfortunately, Albert's present was miserable.

By 1894 Hermann's business was once again failing. He decided he'd have a better chance in a new location and left for Milan, Italy, with Pauline and Maja. Albert pleaded to be allowed to go, but Hermann refused. He wanted his son to graduate from a prestigious high school. After that, Albert was required to serve a hitch in the German army. Just as importantly, Jakob had agreed to finance his nephew's education.

Albert felt abandoned. He hated school, hated the grim boardinghouse where he had to live. Outside of school he was able to compose complex mathematical formulas; in school he was considered an obnoxious discipline problem. One report from that time claimed, "Albert is disruptive and disturbs the other pupils."

Sometimes Albert felt as if he were losing his mind. In 1895 he decided to do just that. He convinced a doctor to write a letter to school officials telling them he was on the verge of a nervous breakdown and needed northern Italy's climate to improve. No one is sure if it was fake or genuine, but the letter, combined with various instructors' complaints about Albert's attitude, convinced the school to let Albert drop out.

Without contacting his parents, Albert boarded a train to Milan. He was 15 and without a high school diploma, but he had a head full of dreams. Somehow, that would have to be enough.

Sometimes aloof, sometimes distant, Albert Einstein's frequent retreats into the world of his own imagination didn't prevent him from keeping friends.

Chapter 3
A Second Chance

· ·

If he expected a pleasant family reunion when he arrived unexpectedly in Milan, Albert Einstein was disappointed. His parents were flabbergasted. Their bright boy, who'd begun his school career at the top of his class, was now a high school dropout. But no matter how much they pleaded and yelled, Albert refused to return to school. His stubbornness was already well developed, and he wouldn't give an inch. He didn't want to be in high school.

His parents weren't alone in their disappointment. Uncle Jakob, who was paying his tuition and living expenses, felt he'd wasted his money.

Hermann suddenly had an inspiration. He'd managed to open a small factory in Milan, and Albert could take a job there. In time he would learn the family business and could even pay back his uncle. There was only one Einstein who disagreed with his solution: Albert. There had to be a better plan than working for his dad.

Albert Einstein soon learned that the Swiss Federal Polytechnic in Zurich, Switzerland, offered admission based solely on test scores—they didn't require a high school diploma. Students who passed the Polytechnic's entrance examinations were automatically admitted.

When Albert told his parents this, he made it sound simple. Unfortunately, like many teens trying to talk their parents into something, Albert had neglected a few details. The main detail, as his mother quickly discovered when she contacted the school, was that test takers had to be 18. The exam was scheduled for the fall—Albert would be 18 months shy of the requirement.

Despite her son's exaggerations, Pauline wanted to support his ambitions. She got in touch with a friend of hers and through his connections arranged a meeting with an admissions counselor at the Polytechnic. Pauline traveled there alone and pleaded her son's case. She was very convincing. She told them about her son's advanced knowledge of physics and produced a letter from one of Albert's gymnasium instructors stating that Albert's mathematical proficiency was equal to that of a student who had graduated.

Pauline made a good case. The Polytechnic made an exception. Despite his youth, Albert could take the exam.

That summer in Milan was idyllic for Albert as he studied for the exams. Without the harsh discipline of school, he was able to let his mind wander down whatever path he chose. He read up on physics and complex mathematics. However, areas that interested him less, like history, French, and biology, received far less attention. The consequences were easily foreseeable. In the fall he took the entrance exams at the Polytechnic and failed miserably. He was refused admission.

Then Albert got a second chance. Reviewing Albert's math and physics scores, Professor Heinrich Weber was astonished. The 16-year-old's scores would have been high for a *college* graduate, let alone someone who'd never finished high school. Weber proposed a solution.

There was good news and bad news. The good news? Albert wouldn't have to take the test over—there would be a spot in the freshman class waiting for him. The bad news? It was a spot in the following year's class. In the meantime, Albert would have to go back to high school.

Although he was disappointed, Albert could recognize a reprieve when he saw one. He enrolled in a high school at Aarau in a German-speaking part of Switzerland. At first he was nervous about returning to high school. Those fears proved unfounded, for while the gymnasium was militaristic, the Swiss school was far more liberal and relaxed. At his new school, Albert was allowed a great deal more academic freedom, and he excelled, earning the equivalent of As in physics, history, and two geometry classes.

The budding scientist found not only a comfortable school in Aarau, but a pleasant new home as well. Jost Winteler, one of the teachers at Albert's new school, gave Albert a place to stay. The Winteler home was happy and carefree, a marked contrast to the Einstein home, which often suffered beneath a choking cloud of financial ruin.

Albert even enjoyed his first romance. Marie Winteler was Jost's 18-year-old daughter. She and Albert began their courtship by playing music together—she on the piano, he on the violin. They quickly began dating, and during the year he spent in the Winteler home, they were often inseparable. By his mid-teens, he was an attractive young man, with thick curly hair, deep eyes and a confident swagger. He wasn't shy, but sometimes he seemed aloof or distracted when he was deep in thought. Throughout Albert's life, this aloof, distracted quality made him even more desirable to many young women.

Though he was well educated, Albert's "attitude" problems often made it difficult for him to get a job, which left him gripped by despair.

Chapter 4
College Life

● ●

For a young talent like Albert Einstein, the Zurich Polytechnic was the best European university outside of Germany. The school was well funded and well equipped. Many of the professors were world renowned, men who had published papers and won awards. Like the Swiss high school he'd attended, the Polytechnic was fairly liberal academically. It even admitted women—a very rare occurrence in the late 19th century.

Albert wasn't on track to become a scientist. His course of study was designed to qualify him to teach math and physics—at the high school level. The class he joined had only five students. Albert would fall in love with one of them.

Mileva Maric was four years older than Albert when the two met; like him, she was majoring in physics. Mileva wasn't classically beautiful, but her intellect fascinated Albert. The two began to meet regularly at local coffeehouses to discuss some of his theories and the classes they shared. Their attraction bloomed slowly; when it did it led to some unfortunate consequences.

The first problem was Mileva's religion. She was Catholic. Einstein didn't care that Mileva wasn't Jewish. Her parents didn't care that Einstein wasn't Catholic. The conflict came from Pauline, who complained about both Mileva's religion and her age, telling Albert his new girlfriend would be "an old hag" by the time he reached 30.

In a letter to Mileva, Albert wrote when he mentioned their marriage plans, "Mama threw herself on the bed, buried her head in the pillow and cried like a child. After she had recovered from the initial shock, she immediately switched to a desperate offensive, 'You are ruining your future and blocking your path through life. That woman cannot gain entrance to a decent family. If she gets a child you'll be in a pretty mess.'"

Although his mother might have been wrong about most things, she was right about the "pretty mess." In 1898 Mileva got pregnant. The couple was completely broke, unmarried and still in college. This would have been a problem in the 21st century; in the 19th it was scandalous. As soon as she found out, Mileva made plans to leave school—although she would take the final exams twice, she never passed them and never earned her degree.

Returning to her native Hungary, Mileva was supported by her parents; she gave birth to a baby girl in February 1899. Although terribly worried, Albert wasn't capable of supporting his new daughter and continued his studies. He did write to Mileva, saying, "I love her so much and I don't even know her yet."

He never would. By most accounts, Albert Einstein's daughter was put up for adoption. Despite the event, when Mileva returned to school, the couple continued to date.

Albert focused on "self education"—formal classes proved to be as boring to him at the Polytechnic as they'd been in the gymnasium. He cut classes regularly, relying on either Mileva or fellow classmate Marcel Grossmann to lend him their notes. At the Polytechnic, the only real requirement was that Albert pass the main examinations, given in the second and the fourth (final) year. Despite his low attendance, on the second-year exams, Albert beat the other four members of his class.

Albert's refusal to attend most of his professors' lectures didn't win him any popularity contests—his math professor called him "a lazy dog," and even Heinrich Weber, who'd fought to get Albert admitted to the Polytechnic early, probably regretted the decision. The few times Albert attended Weber's physics class the two argued, once over Weber's refusal to discuss James Maxwell (one of Albert's favorite scientists) and another time over Weber's refusal to allow Albert to perform experiments on "the ether."

But Albert Einstein was not a lazy dog. He just preferred to do independent research. He would once write that curiosity "stands mainly in need of freedom, without which it goes to wreck and ruin without fail."

Of course most physics majors need teachers. But then, Albert was not like most physics majors. By the time of his final exams, he was already contemplating ideas that few of his peers would even understand. However, if he was advanced in some areas, his final scores didn't prove it—he earned a 4.91 out of 6.0 and was beaten by three other classmates. Only Mileva, who failed with a four out of six, had a lower score.

"For the exams, one had to stuff oneself with all this rubbish," Albert later complained, "whether one wanted to or not. This conclusion had such a negative effect on me that after my finals, the consideration of any scientific problem was distasteful for me for a whole year."

After graduation, Einstein quickly learned the price of skipping classes and coming across as arrogant. None of his former professors wanted to hire him. Albert desperately wanted a job as an assistant, but those he approached weren't interested. Even Heinrich Weber, who as a physics professor was Albert's best choice, hired two mechanical engineers rather than Albert, even though he'd majored in the subject and the engineers had little lab experience.

While no one was willing to pay him, another physics professor, the University of Zurich's Dr. Alfred Kleiner, gave Albert the chance to do doctoral work. Unfortunately the paper Albert wrote wasn't accepted—no one at the university could understand it. Albert eventually withdrew it, because he needed to get back the 200 francs he'd paid in submission fees. Some of that initial thesis would later become part of his special theory of relativity.

While there were many challenges, Albert did have one success that year—he published a paper in a very well known science magazine. Unfortunately its publication didn't lead to new opportunities, and what Albert needed, more than anything else, was money.

At 22, Albert was forced to return to Milan. He had very little to show for his time in Zurich, other than his newly won Swiss citizenship. His father's business was failing (again), and he could offer little help. But when Hermann Einstein learned his son had sent Professor Wilhelm Ostwald the science article he'd written, Hermann wrote the professor a letter. "My son feels profoundly unhappy with his present lack of position," Albert's father explained, "and his idea that he has gone off the tracks with his career and is now out of touch gets more and more entrenched every day."

Despite the two Einsteins' efforts, Professor Ostwald never responded. By then, Albert had gotten used to rejection.

He'd taken a temporary teaching job, but that ended after three months. He took a job as a math tutor but was fired for insolence. It was a good thing he had an escape into the imaginary world of numbers and theories, because the real world was becoming a huge challenge.

Even his girlfriend, Mileva, was losing faith in him, writing in a letter to a friend, "Albert has not got a position. . . . You can imagine he does not feel good in such a state of dependency [on his parents]. Yet, it is not likely that he will soon get a secure position, you know that my sweetheart has a very wicked tongue and is a Jew in the bargain."

Whether or not anti-Semitic—or anti-Jewish—feelings held Albert Einstein back in the early portions of his career is debatable. What isn't is that the one job he was finally offered took nearly a year to get. His old classmate at the Polytechnic, Marcel Grossmann, used a family connection to get Albert a job interview at the patent office in Bern. Albert's job would be reviewing patent applications and seeing if the drawings of the wannabe inventors matched their descriptions, and if the invention was even possible. It was a good job for someone like Einstein, someone who was able to look at a sheet of paper filled with lines and numbers and turn it into something in his head. Although the job was usually filled by engineers, the patent office's director, Friedrich Haller, was impressed enough with Albert's educational background to promise the recent college graduate a job interview.

After nearly a year, Albert was finally offered the job. In June 1902, one of the world's greatest scientists was offered a paltry 3,500 francs a year to become a Technical Expert Class III. Although the position was on a trial basis, by then he was glad to take it.

Albert Einstein's best known theories were developed when he was a young man. However, he would not be respected as a scientist until he was much older.

Chapter 5

A Very Good Year

• •

An astronaut gets on a rocket ship, one capable of traveling close to the speed of light. His wife stays behind on Earth. The clocks on the astronaut's ship show that a year has passed. But when he returns home, 20 years have passed. Science fiction? No, just one of the amazing conclusions reached from Albert Einstein's theory of relativity.

What is almost as astonishing is that he came up with most of his main theories during a single "miracle year" when he was only 26.

In June 1902, when he was 23, Albert Einstein began working at the patent office in Bern, Switzerland. Some descriptions of him from this time are of a rather lackadaisical man who spent most of his workday dreaming up bizarre new theories. This simply wasn't true. Albert's position at the patent office was very demanding. It required that he try to make sense of the notes and diagrams that accompanied the applications submitted by dreamers, many of whom had little scientific or engineering background. So, although his job as a clerk might seem to have been a million miles away from a job as an assistant to a university professor, it actually required similar intellectual ability.

Away from work his relationship with Mileva was moving forward, although some part of this was due to a family tragedy. In 1902, Einstein's father died of a heart attack. Left widowed, Pauline suddenly put up less resistance to her son's engagement to Mileva, and in January 1903 the two were wed. A year later the couple's first son, Hans Albert, was born.

Although their cramped apartment at 49 Kramgasse, which was described by one visitor as hot and reeking from the smell of diapers and Albert's pipe tobacco, wasn't the ideal place for one of the greatest minds of the 20th century to construct his theories, by all accounts Albert did much of his work there. Often he would be reading a difficult text while absentmindedly rocking Hans' cradle as the infant bawled.

Outside his home, Albert founded the Olympia Academy. Despite the highfalutin title, it was really just a group of men with an interest in physics discussing the latest theories. It also gave Albert an opportunity to explore his own ideas out loud. One of the men who joined the group was Michele Besso, an engineer whom Einstein helped land a job at the patent office. Besso was a good listener and as an engineer asked different questions than a physicist might.

After some struggle, in 1905 Albert finally received his doctorate from the University of Zurich. Getting the degree seemed to free Albert's mind for loftier work. Since none of the academics at the university had understood his first submission, he'd focused his doctoral thesis in 1905 on molecules.

He was now Albert Einstein, Ph.D., and although he was still a patent clerk, he was able to begin the most important work of his life.

In a letter to Conrad Habicht, Albert Einstein gave a hint of what he was considering: "the radiation and energy of light . . . the methods of determining the real dimensions of atoms . . . random motion [of small bodies in liquid] due to thermal motor of molecules . . . the concepts of electrodynamics of moving bodies, which employs a modification of the theory of space and time." It was this last sentence, the "modification of space and time," that would fundamentally alter scientists' view of the universe.

Albert Einstein's theories can be traced back to the work of three men, men who lived centuries before Einstein. The first, Nicolaus Copernicus, in the 1500s challenged the prevailing theory that Earth was at the center of the universe. This was in many ways the beginning of what became a scientific revolution. Copernicus believed Earth orbited the sun. The religious leaders of the period called his ideas heresy—against the church. This was because he suggested that our planet, which they considered God's creation, was not the universe's center. Besides, his critics asked, if Earth were really moving, why didn't birds get left behind every time they took flight?

Four centuries before Einstein lived, Nicolaus Copernicus revolutionized science by challenging the prevailing theories of the time.

In the 1600s, Galileo Galilei, a supporter of Copernican theory, conducted his own experiment to prove Copernicus right. Galileo lived in Venice, Italy, and he took full advantage of the city's canals and sailing ships. One day he took a boat out; once it reached a constant speed he dropped weights from the top of its mast. As he'd expected, the weights dropped straight down, hitting the ship's deck. According to critics of Copernicus, the weights should have fallen into the water (since the boat was moving forward, and thus out from under the falling weight).

What Galileo had demonstrated was that in a boat (or any vehicle for that matter), it didn't matter if it was at rest or in motion. As long as it moved at a constant speed (without acceleration or deceleration), any activity that could be performed on the boat at rest could be performed with the same result when it was in motion. It also didn't matter

Galileo Galilei was able to create experiments that proved Copernican theories. He also developed his own revolutionary theories.

whether the water was moving and the ship was at rest, or the ship was moving and the water was at rest. What mattered was only the "relative" motion of one to the other.

In science, proving a respected scientist's theories incorrect is like a star athlete breaking a sports record. For Albert Einstein, that competitor was Sir Isaac Newton. Newton's miracle year occurred in 1665, when Newton was 23 and had left Cambridge University to avoid the plague. He called his theories "laws" because he believed they were true and unbreakable throughout the universe. Some of Newton's laws came through simple observation—he crafted his law of gravity after being hit on the head by an apple. Other laws such as the law of inertia were more complicated. This law describes how all objects resist change in motion; it's still applied today, such as whenever the space shuttle or a missile is launched.

The laws that Albert's writings disproved were Newton's principles of absolute time and absolute space.

"Absolute, true and mathematical time, of itself, and from its own nature flows equably without relation to anything external and by another name is called duration," Newton wrote in his most famous publication, *Principia.* Newton believed nothing affected absolute time, and that it was possible to measure the exact location and time of an object in space. Einstein believed Newton was wrong; he believed that by measuring one, the other would be affected.

Generally Albert respected Newton as a scientist, writing in the foreword to the 1931 edition of Newton's *Opticks,* "[N]ature to him was an open book, whose letters he could read without effort." However, Albert Einstein had no problem disputing his theories. He believed one thing would contradict Newton's law of absolute time: light. In Newton's time—the 1670s—Danish astronomer Olaus Rømer approximated the speed of light by studying the movement of one of Jupiter's moons. In 1849, Armand Fizeau came up with a more accurate measurement. Light travels at 186,281 miles per second. The questions puzzling scientists were: Is this an absolute speed? Was the speed of light unchanging, supporting Newton's theories about absolute time and absolute space?

In 1886, Ernst Mach broke the so-called sound barrier by firing projectiles that exceeded the speed of sound in air (this is where Mach numbers come from—"Mach two" is twice the speed of sound.) Mach's experiments flowed easily with Newtonian theory. An object should be able to reach any rate of speed as long as the needed force is supplied. Just as the sound barrier had been broken, many scientists in Einstein's time believed the light barrier could be broken.

They were wrong.

In 1868, James Clerk Maxwell produced the first complete theory describing both how light was produced and how this related to how fast it moved. He was also the first to note that light traveled through waves of "ether." Maxwell's theories fascinated Albert Einstein; he'd read about them as a teen and begged Professor Weber at Zurich Polytechnic to allow him to re-create Maxwell's experiments and prove their validity.

While he wasn't allowed to conduct such an experiment, two American scientists did test Maxwell's theories. In 1886, Edward Morley and Albert Abraham Michelson created an

When Ernst Mach (left) broke the sound barrier, most scientists believed the light barrier would someday be broken as well. James Maxwell (right) performed experiments that Einstein found fascinating. Maxwell's experiments led Einstein to prove the light barrier was unbreakable.

experiment designed to show how light is affected by the ether. At the time, scientists believed the ether flowed in a certain direction, and thus would create resistance when light traveled along it. Morley and Michelson believed by reflecting beams of light from mirrors facing in both the direction ether was thought to move and in the opposite direction, they would be able to record minute variations in the speed of light. In other words, light would slow down when it went against the ether.

Light didn't slow down. No matter what scientists did, they could not affect the speed of light; they could not make it go any faster or slower.

How light traveled had been one of Albert's first thought experiments, at 16, when he imagined what it would be like to travel on a beam of light. Light's speed, and whether or not it was a constant, would become his focus of study in early 1905—Albert Einstein's "miracle year."

In a fairly straightforward series of papers published in 1905, Einstein disproved the existence of the ether. There is some question as to how aware Einstein was of the Michelson-Morley experiments in 1905, but he did mention how experiments conducted in the late 1800s proved that light's speed is a constant. Nothing can make it go slower; nothing can make it go faster.

This simple statement had tremendous implications.

Imagine that you are traveling in a spaceship through the darkness of space. Traveling faster than any spaceship in history, it is cruising at close to the speed of light: 185,281 miles per second. You decide to turn on your spaceship's headlight so that you can see.

Now consider an observer watching as you do this. The observer has a device to measure both your speed and the speed of light as it escapes from the spaceship's headlight. So how much faster is that beam of light traveling than your spaceship?

The obvious answer would seem to be one thousand miles per second faster. But according to Einstein this is wrong. Since light travels at a constant rate of speed, it wouldn't appear to leave your spaceship at only 1,000 miles per second. It would travel at 186,281 miles per second—that's how fast you would see it travel from inside your spaceship, and that's how fast an observer on the ground would see it travel. But how can this be?

The answer is that if light speed is constant, then something else must be flexible. In Einstein's theories, that something is time. That is why for someone inside a spaceship approaching the speed of light, time would slow down. In a way, travel that fast is an anti-aging device.

In later years, Albert Einstein jokingly explained this time change by saying, "When you are courting a nice girl an hour seems like a second. When you sit on a red hot cinder a second seems like an hour. That's relativity."

Einstein's theories of relativity attempted to prove the following:

1) The speed of light is unchanging.

2) Nothing can travel faster than the speed of light.

3) The faster an object travels, the more its mass increases (if an object's speed were to approach the speed of light, it would become too heavy to propel).

4) Relativity occurs in a four-dimensional world of height, length, breadth, and time.

5) Time changes depending on how quickly or slowly something is moving.

Albert Einstein's theories, explained in four articles published during 1905, would eventually revolutionize physics, and the way the universe is viewed. But in the beginning no one noticed. By the end of 1905, Albert Einstein, Ph.D., was still a struggling patent clerk.

Looking unusually sharp and stylish, a young Albert Einstein prepares a lecture.

Chapter 6
Respect

. . . .

The first few years after Albert Einstein's "miracle year" of 1905 were difficult. He'd published four papers. The least well known examined the size of a sugar molecule. Another examined how light can behave as either a wave or a particle (like a gas), depending on the circumstances. This theory wouldn't be accepted for over a decade, but it would lead to the development of television. The other two papers examined "special relativity." They too would not be accepted for some time. Because his three major papers were so little understood, Einstein did not receive the flood of offers from universities that he'd anticipated. Still, he was good at his job in the patent office and received several promotions.

He spent the next two years working through the implications of what would be his most famous formula. Einstein paid for all those math classes he'd skipped in college. His mathematics background was spotty, and much of his time on the formula was spent figuring out the math. Despite its complexity, it is a very elegant and simple-looking equation—probably the most famous formula in history: $E = mc^2$.

In this formula E is energy, m is mass, and c is the speed of light. Einstein's formula shows that matter—or mass—is really solidified energy. It would take just a small amount of matter to release a tremendous amount of energy. This formula explains how our sun has been able to produce heat and light for billions of years. It has also been used to truly devastating effect.

It wasn't until 1909 that Albert Einstein was able to work as a full-time professor, when he was hired by the University of Zurich. From the beginning, Einstein was an unusual professor. Most professors would arrive at their class, give an organized lecture and leave. Albert Einstein would come in with a scrap or two of paper on which he'd jotted some general idea for his class lecture. Often he'd stray quickly from that topic, instead answering students' questions and conducting more of a physics conversation than a structured class. Afterward, he'd join his students at a local coffee shop or even invite them to his home. For many of the students it was a great way to learn; years later they'd recall Albert Einstein as their favorite teacher.

By the time of his first professorship, Einstein's papers were being studied by the top minds of the time, and he began receiving letters from them. They were filled with questions. For the most part Einstein enjoyed the debate his ideas encouraged—at least someone was finally noticing his work. While the theories still attracted skepticism from many, there was little doubt about the genius of the man who'd crafted them.

In 1911, Albert Einstein joined the faculty of the University of Prague. The next year he became a professor at the Zurich Polytechnic, and in 1914 he took a position at the University of Berlin. On every move he made, his wife and children followed (his second son, Eduard, was born in 1910).

However, his appointment to the University of Berlin shattered the already fragile bonds of the Einstein marriage. Mileva hated Berlin, missed Zurich, and decided she'd had enough. She left Albert, returning to Switzerland with their children. The two would not be divorced until 1919, but the marriage was over.

As part of the divorce agreement, Albert pledged to give Mileva the money if he won the Nobel Prize, the most prestigious award in science. At the time this was seen as a noble gesture on the part of a man who wanted to support his ex-wife and children. However, since then there has been considerable speculation that the promise represented much, much more. Mileva had of course been a physics major, and some believe that it was his discussions with her and not the Olympia Academy that helped him create his famous formulas. While it has never been proven, some believe Albert Einstein would never have come up with his theories without his wife's help.

Unlike many scientists who prefer writing books and working in the lab over teaching, Einstein was an adept and popular professor.

In 1915, Albert Einstein published his "General Theory of Relativity." While earlier work had questioned Newton's laws of absolute time and absolute space, this theory questioned Newton's law of gravity. Einstein proposed that gravity didn't cause Earth's orbital movement; instead it was because our sun caused the space around it to curve. Einstein predicted how the curved space around our sun could be observed; he claimed that the light rays from distant stars would actually bend as they passed by our sun.

This notion of curved space was considered even more radical than his earlier theories. But there was a way to prove it. Four years later during a solar eclipse, when the sun's light was blocked by the moon and the sky darkened, two scientists—Andrew Crommelin and Arthur Eddington— took pictures of stars normally visible only at night. When

As an astronomy professor, Arthur Eddington didn't just believe Einstein's theories, he helped prove them.

they examined these photos and compared them to earlier pictures of the stars, it looked as if they had "jumped" sideways. The stars hadn't really moved, of course. Their light was bent. Albert Einstein was right. His earlier theories had brought him some renown, but his theory of general relativity made him an international superstar. He was photographed and interviewed in the major magazines of the time; he was stopped on the street for his autograph.

By then he was also developing an image as an eccentric— a very bright but very unusual man. He hated wearing socks, his clothes were usually wrinkled; he was reported to have owned a dozen identical suits so that he'd never have to think about what to wear in the morning. One story described the genius scientist being asked for his phone number. Albert had to look it up. "You don't know your own phone number?" the man asked. "Why should I memorize something which is easily found?" Albert is reported to have replied.

There would be one other, major verification of an Einstein theory in his lifetime. The consequences from the test of his famous formula, $E = mc^2$, would sometimes make him wish he'd never written it in the first place.

After German President Paul von Hindenburg (left) gave Adolf Hitler authority to form a new government, Hitler and the Nazis suspended many freedoms, sent non-Aryans to concentration camps, and invaded several countries. World War II was just around the corner.

Chapter 7

Wars

• •

World War I, or the Great War, which started with the assassination of an archduke and his wife and ended with millions killed or wounded, eventually affected much of Europe and involved the United States and Canada. As a citizen of a neutral country—Switzerland—Albert Einstein wasn't involved with Germany's war effort. However, he hated war and its tragic consequences and spent much of his time during the period fighting for peace. He added his signature to the "Manifesto to Europeans," which called for an end to war in 1915.

Five years later, after the war's conclusion, Albert Einstein himself would be the focus of protests in Berlin by German citizens who believed he'd betrayed his homeland. Germany by then was a defeated country, suffering from national poverty. It was also experiencing an increase in anti-Semitism, or hatred toward Jewish people. This hatred would help Adolf Hitler's rise to chancellor of Germany. Hitler, with his Nazi party, would lead Germany into another world war and kill millions of Jews.

For Albert the post–World War I years were a contrast as his career and personal life grew more successful, even as his religion was under attack. In 1919 he'd married his cousin Elsa Löwenthal, who'd nursed him to health during a serious illness two years before. He'd also become a director for the prestigious Kaiser Wilhelm Institute in Berlin.

In 1921 Albert's professional success reached its peak when he was awarded the Nobel Prize in physics. Although

Elsa Löwenthal, Albert's second wife, made sure the absent-minded professor wore clean clothes and kept his appointments.

a very prestigious award, it was given to him for what is now considered a lesser theory, his paper on the photoelectric effect of light. Many believe the reason for this was because his theories of relativity were controversial and still not well understood by even the top physicists. As promised, he sent the $32,000 award to his ex-wife.

It is during this time that Albert Einstein labored to relate all of the properties of matter into a "unified field theory." This work would consume the rest of his life, but he would find little success. While Newton had found God intimately responsible for the workings of the universe, as Einstein grew older, he imagined a precisely crafted universe—one in which everything fits neatly into place. As he told physicist Neils Bohr, "I am convinced that God does not play dice."

In the 1920s and '30s, Einstein also became more connected to his Jewish roots. He began to support Zionist causes, which called for a Jewish state, and he put his energy into fighting the prejudice many German Jews were experiencing. In 1933, Germany's President Paul von Hindenburg gave Adolf Hitler authority to form a new government, and soon after Hitler was given "emergency powers." Free speech and free press were eliminated. Hitler's "Final Solution" called for the eventual extermination of all non-Aryans—people such as the Jews, Gypsies, and Catholics. These people were restricted in their movement and were regularly assaulted by Nazi supporters. More than 6 million civilians would die at the hands of the Nazis.

Among the Nazis, Jewish scientists were hated more than any other professionals. Nazi Nobel laureate Phillipp von Lenard had done work on the photoelectric effect before Einstein and was upset that Einstein was able to formulate a law explaining it. He called Einstein "the most important example of the dangerous influence of Jewish circles on the study of nature." A 20,000-mark reward was offered by the Nazis to anyone who killed Einstein. "I didn't know I was worth so much," he would later joke, but the threat was no laughing matter.

In 1932, Albert Einstein left Europe for an American lecture tour. He would not go back. Instead he took a position at Princeton University in Princeton, New Jersey, the next year. Although he would keep his Swiss citizenship, he would also become a citizen of the United States.

As he learned more and more about the horrors Jewish people were experiencing in Germany, his position about peace changed: "Organized power can be opposed only by organized power," he admitted during World War II.

In 1936, Albert's second wife, Elsa, died. She had been the one who made sure he was organized when he left for his lectures, and that his rumpled clothes were kept clean. After her death, Albert became more of a loner but continued to teach and conduct research on his unified field theory.

Back in Germany, Otto Hahn and his assistant, Fritz Strassmann, began experimenting with a new type of weapon, one that through nuclear fission would release the energy Einstein described in his formula $E = mc^2$. In the United States, Hahn's former partner, Lise Meitner, relying

In Germany, Otto Hahn (left) embarked on experiments using Einstein's formulas as his former partner, Lise Meitner (right) conducted similar research in the United States.

in part on Einstein's famous equation, would calculate its potential. A single gram of uranium, under the right conditions, could release as much energy as many pounds of dynamite. The Germans were building the most dangerous weapon in human history—the atomic bomb.

Learning of the discovery, Edward Teller, a physicist, went to Einstein and convinced him to write the letter that led the United States to develop its own atomic bomb. On August 2, 1939, in a letter to President Franklin Roosevelt, Albert Einstein explained the significance of the German experiments. "This new phenomenon would also lead to the construction of bombs. . . . A single bomb of this type, carried

Edward Teller, later known as the father of the hydrogen bomb, here testifies before Congress about the atomic bomb's potential.

The deadliest weapon ever designed, the atomic bomb would not have been possible without Einstein's theories. Though the bomb killed tens of thousands of people, it saved many more lives by ending World War II.

by boat and exploded in a port, might well destroy the whole port together with some of the surrounding territory."

By the 1940s, Germany, Russia, and the United States were all in a race: a race to build the first atomic bomb.

When the United States entered the war following a surprise attack on Pearl Harbor by German ally Japan on December 7, 1941, the effort to design an atomic bomb was already under way. Germany surrendered on May 7, 1945. They never built an atomic bomb. However, Japan was still a threat.

The first successful test of an atomic bomb took place on July 16, 1945, at a test site called Trinity, 200 miles south of Los Alamos, New Mexico. It was an awesome sight: a mushroom-shaped cloud billowed 40,000 feet over the desert sky, blinding light flashed below and the ground shook violently.

The single blast was the equivalent of the force in more than 20,000 tons of dynamite. Many involved believed if the Japanese could have seen what they had just witnessed, the war would effectively be over. A number of them lobbied government officials to demonstrate the weapon's power over an isolated, unpopulated area of Japan. Surely once Japanese officials realized how powerful the weapon was, they'd give up.

Other scientists and new President Harry S. Truman disagreed. They felt they had three choices: a ground invasion, a demonstration, or an actual bombing. A ground invasion could cost thousands of American soldiers their lives. A mere demonstration was considered too risky for other reasons.

Albert Einstein wasn't consulted. He'd later say that if he'd known the Germans would never get the bomb, he wouldn't have encouraged the United States to pursue the weapon.

An atomic weapon was loaded into the bomb bay of the *Enola Gay,* the plane chosen to deliver this deadly cargo. On August 6, 1945, the plane flew over Japan, dropping the atomic bomb on the city of Hiroshima. The destructive power of that bomb, and the one that followed it at Nagasaki three days later, vaporized buildings and killed over 150,000 people in single blasts of heat and light. Just as many would die later from illnesses caused by radiation.

Japan surrendered on August 14.

After World War II Albert Einstein would once again work for peace. He called for the atomic bomb to be declared illegal. He also hoped to see the destructive power demonstrated by the atomic bomb used for energy instead.

In 1950, Einstein published a paper describing his unified field theory. While he'd earned a great deal of respect for his earlier theories, his new ideas were ignored. The next year he was offered the presidency of the newly formed Jewish State of Israel. He declined.

After several years of chronic health problems, Albert Einstein died on April 18, 1955. Today more of his theories have been verified. Some have been used to explain everything from black holes—stars 10,000 times the size of our sun whose implosion creates such a strong spatial curve that even light cannot escape—and wormholes, possible passages in space that may be used to traverse both time and light-years of space in a millisecond.

"For the most part I do the thing which my own nature drives me to do," Albert Einstein once explained. "It is embarrassing to earn so much respect and love for it. Arrows of hate have been shot at me, too; but they never hit me, because somehow they belong to another world, with which I have no connection whatsoever." By living in his own world, a world of his own mind, Albert Einstein changed everyone else's view of our world forever.

Albert Einstein Chronology

1879 Albert Einstein is born on March 14 in Ulm, Germany

1889 Enters the Luitpold Gymnasium

1895 Drops out of Luitpold Gymnasium; is rejected by Swiss Federal Polytechnic in Zurich, Switzerland; attends high school in Aarau; is accepted to Polytechnic for the next year

1899 Mileva Maric and Albert have a daughter; she is believed to be put up for adoption

1900 Graduates Polytechnic; becomes engaged to Mileva Maric; first scientific paper is published

1901 Obtains Swiss citizenship

1902 Begins working in Bern, Switzerland, patent office

1903 On January 6, Albert and Mileva are married

1904 First son, Hans Albert, is born

1905 The "miracle year"—Einstein publishes several important papers, two on special relativity; earns his Ph.D. from the university of Zurich

1910 On July 28, second son, Eduard, is born

1911 Albert becomes a professor at the University of Prague

1912 Takes a job as a full professor at the Zurich Polytechnic

1914 The Einsteins relocate to Berlin, where Albert works as a professor at Berlin University; soon after, Mileva and the children return to Zurich

1919 Einstein divorces Mileva, marries Elsa Löwenthal; becomes director of Kaiser Wilhelm Institute

1921 Wins Nobel Prize in physics

1929 Receives one of physics' highest honors—the Planck Medal

1932 Accepts a position at Princeton University in Princeton, New Jersey, and permanently moves to the United States

1933 Becomes professor at the Institute for Advanced Study in Princeton, New Jersey

1936 Elsa Einstein dies

1940 Becomes a United States citizen

1955 On April 18, dies in the Princeton Hospital

Time Line of Discovery

1514 Nicolaus Copernicus circulates an outline of his theory about Earth revolving around the sun

1600s Galileo Galilei conducts experiments relating to Copernican theory

1665 Twenty-four-year-old Isaac Newton formulates his laws of gravity, space, and time

1670s Speed of light determined by Danish astronomer Olaus Rømer using eclipse of Jupiter's moons

1849 Armand Fizeau determines speed of light

1873 James Clerk Maxwell suggests experiments to determine Earth's absolute motion through space and develops theory of the ether

1886 Edward Morley and Albert Abraham Michelson's experiment designed to show how light is affected by the ether shows light's speed is constant

1905 Albert Einstein publishes two papers on his theory of special relativity showing how the speed limit of light affects time

1915 Einstein publishes his "General Theory of Relativity," proposing that Earth's movement through space is the result of our sun causing the space around it to curve

1919 During a solar eclipse Andrew Crommelin and Arthur Eddington's star photos show light is bent, proving Einstein's theory

1938 Otto Hahn with Lise Meitner, then with Fritz Strassmann, discover nuclear fission

Further Reading

Books

Bernstein, Jeremy. *Albert Einstein and the Frontiers of Physics.* New York: Oxford University Press, 1996.

MacDonald, Fiona. *Albert Einstein: Genius Behind the Theory of Relativity.* Woodbridge, Conn.: Blackbirch Press, 2000.

Parker, Barry. *Einstein's Brainchild.* Amherst, New York: Prometheus, 2000.

Strathern, Paul. *The Big Idea: Einstein and Relativity.* New York: Random House, 1997.

White, Michael. *Isaac Newton: Discovering Laws that Govern the Universe.* Woodbridge, Conn.: Blackbirch Press, 1999.

On the Web:

www.aip.org/history/einstein/
www.devine-ent.com
www.Nobel.se/physics/laureates/1921/
www.pbs.org

Glossary of Terms

· ·

absolute motion—Motion that does not change no matter what system it's measured in.

absolute time—Time that does not change regardless of an observer's motion in the universe.

acceleration—Rate of change of velocity.

black hole—An area in space, usually the result of a star's collapse, in which the gravitational field is so strong, even light cannot escape.

ether—Substance once believed to carry light waves; proven nonexistent by Einstein.

implosion—Inward collapse.

inertia—Resistance to change or motion.

mass—The amount of matter in an object.

wormhole—Warped space leading toward a black hole.

Index